LAMBORGHINI COUNTACH

Graham Robson

BEEKMAN HOUSE
New York

Louis Weber, President
Publications International, Ltd.
3841 West Oakton Street
Skokie, Illinois 60076

This 1986 edition published by Beekman House,
distributed by Crown Publishers, Inc.

ISBN: 0-517-62731-0

Printed and bound in Yugoslavia
h g f e d c b a

Contents

Credits

Photography and illustration were provided by: Ing. Bruno Fiumana and Jonathan Schwitz of Agostini Autojunior—61; Andrea Hogrefe of Alpine Electronics of America—*34, 41, 63; Dr. Gian Panicco and Elizabetta Farmeschi of Carrozzeria Bertone S.p.A.—17, 20, 21, 42, 43, 44; Micro Decet—46; Mitch Frumkin—7, 36, 59; David Gooley—12, 14, 15, 16; Harry Hobbs—47, 48, 49, 50, 51; Art LeFebvre & Associates—40, 45; Randy Lorentzen—pages 4, 5; Doug Mitchel—28, 30, 36, 37, 59; Frank Ritota of Model Rectifier Corporation—63, Ubaldo Sgarzi of Nuova Automobili Ferruccio Lamborghini S.p.A.—*6, 8, 9, 10, 11, 13, 15, 19, 21, 37, 54, 55, 56, 57; Steve Russell of Pirelli Tire Corporation—*62; Positive Image—57; Franco B. Rossi—23, 24, 25, 26, 27, 28, 29, 30, 31, 32, 33, 38, 39; Ken Sullivan—*35, 52, 53, 58, 60, 61. *indicates cover photo credit

Countach:
The Standard for Exotic Cars

The point can be made that only a few truly exotic cars are built in the world. Further, the high cost of materials, performance, and craftsmanship puts these super automobiles out of the reach of everyone but the wealthy. Surely Lamborghini's Countach qualifies as one of the exotic, no matter how the elements of exotica are defined. In fact, its features themselves set the standards by which other exotic cars could be judged.

A Countach will cause a commotion wherever it is driven. Its styling is shocking. Its manner is bullish. Its performance is astounding. Not enough superlatives exist to describe the effect of Lamborghini's accomplishments in this mid-engine missile over the last 15 or so years. While its performance may be challenged by other makes, the Countach is unique enough in its many other facets to have endured—and even prevailed.

The Lamborghini Countach gives us permission to fantasize, because the car is a fantasy in its own right. With its wings, spoilers, tires, powerplant, and beetle-wing doors, the Countach has to be from another time, another dimension. It must be someone else's dream into which we have stumbled—a fantastic dream come to life, making its mark even beyond the automotive world by capturing the fancy of countless admirers through posters, models, and advertising campaigns for a variety of products.

Improbable as it may appear sitting next to vehicles built to satisfy ordinary transportation needs, the Countach is, indeed, a firm reality, born through the efforts of earthbound designers and engineers. The genesis of the Countach follows, tracing the history of how this otherworldly car emerged out of a company besieged by very worldly concerns and problems—a shining star piercing the

shroud of everyday business gone awry—to become the world's foremost super auto.

Exotic, super, fantastic, improbable, incredible—these are only words, and words can give but a hint of what something that exists in three dimensions can be like. While driving a Countach is an experience in reality that few drivers are likely to share, the Countach is a delight to enthusiasts by virtue of its presence, its existence. The ultimate automotive fantasy, the Countach is Ferruccio Lamborghini's dream come true. The Countach has become both the standard for the world's exotic cars and an inspiration for all who dream dreams of their own.

Ferruccio Lamborghini: The Man and His Dreams

The popular tale that used to be told was that Ferruccio Lamborghini was unhappy with his Ferraris, or that Enzo Ferrari himself had treated Lamborghini badly. So, being not only a proud Italian but also a self-made millionaire besides, Lamborghini decided to fight back in the best possible way—he would build better, faster, sexier cars of his own! The story is a good one, whether or not it is true, given Lamborghini's nature. Should you ever have met him in person, you would quickly come to the conclusion that the story could have happened that way, because Ferruccio was, and is, a man of great passions and great enthusiasms who would certainly not have liked being treated in the same manner as Ferrari's other "subjects."

Let's put the story into perspective, bearing in mind some facts about the man Ferruccio Lamborghini. He was already rich before founding the Lamborghini automobile business, and he was certainly a Ferrari owner. He had a passion for truly fast and exciting cars, as all normal Italians seem to have, and he could see how making a

new marque distinctive and attractive was possible. So he did: In 1963, the first Lamborghini prototype was built, and a new automotive legend began. Clearly, everything involved with the eventual birth of the Countach was influenced by what had gone before. Without the early Lamborghini enterprises, Automobili Ferruccio Lamborghini would never have been founded, nor would the Countach eventually have seen the light of day.

Ferruccio Lamborghini was not always well-to-do. In fact, the stocky, powerful-looking Emilian was born in 1918 to a farming family in Renazzo di Cento, a small rural village not far to the north of Bologna. The village was, of course, in the valley of the river Po, where the people always seem to be possessed with automobiles and other high-speed machinery. Perhaps it was no coincidence that Maserati established itself in Bologna in the Twenties and that Ferrari's cars evolved close to Modena, only about 25 miles away. By the Thirties, when Lamborghini was in his teens, Italy's race cars were more successful than any in the

Opposite page: A picture of Ferruccio Lamborghini from a few years ago shows a man of great passions and great enthusiasms. His industrial successes began with the production of tractors, then fuel oil burners and air conditioners. Finally, he had the Countach—the most fabulous of supercars—developed. Above: The Lamborghini automobile manufacturing plant as it looks today. Ferruccio Lamborghini built the plant exclusively for making high-performance automobiles, keeping the production centers of all of his ventures separate.

world, except for those of Germany, and Ferruccio was infected with an enthusiasm for cars of all types. His parents realized that they would never make a farmer of him until his passions for machinery were harnessed, and they sent him off to a technical high school. From there he only took a short step to joining the Italian Army for World War II, helping to look after a transport pool of vehicles.

Ferruccio Lamborghini the entrepreneur surfaced immediately after the war. Yard by yard, Italy's land was bitterly disputed by opposing forces between 1943 and 1945. The country was exhausted and seemed to be suffering from massive shortages of virtually everything. The Lamborghini family's greatest need was for a tractor, but such things simply were not available. The resourceful Ferruccio, who had spent the war years on Rhodes keeping vehicles running despite a shortage of parts, cast about in

wrecking yards and war surplus depots, managing to assemble an engine here, a transmission there, and a back axle somewhere else. The result: the very first Lamborghini tractor, put together in haste and with little science involved.

In 1949, the Lamborghini Trattrice was founded in Cento, and before long the tractor manufacturing business expanded to a production rate of about 25 units every day. Within a decade, Lamborghini was a rich man, but he was restless to accomplish even more. In 1960, he decided to start making industrial and domestic fuel oil burners, an enterprise that would become the Lamborghini Bruciatori business at Pieve di Cento, still very close to Cento itself and to Lamborghini's own home. Soon, the factory was also producing air-conditioning units. Ferruccio Lamborghini was on his way to making a second fortune.

Now Ferruccio Lamborghini de-

cided that he could at last turn to his first love—automobiles. A comment by Rob de la Rive Box and Richard Crump from an earlier study of Lamborghini cars: "It would have been possible in the early 1960s for Lamborghini to acquire either a majority shareholding in a small car constructor, or purchase outright a coach-building company, through which he could push **his** ideas on a proven rolling chassis. Neither 'buying-in' approach appealed to this energetic businessman. His **own** car, displayed at the 1963 Turin Motor Show [which opened in November], was the first result of his single-minded attitude to be designer/constructor himself." Ferruccio had already made his first moves into the automobile business before the end of 1962, when he had bought a "greenfield" factory site at Sant'Agata Bolognese, which was a village well off the main road between Bologna and Modena, almost halfway

between Modena and Renazzo di Cento. Although the completed building intended for car manufacturing occupied 500,000 square feet, the first prototype automobile took shape in Lamborghini's tractor facility.

Lamborghini was no designer— merely a well-heeled enthusiast—so all automotive expertise had to be brought into the company. The whole car had to be new, and Lamborghini was determined that it should outshine Ferrari in every way. As with Ferrari development, the entire design had to center around the engine. But who to hire for such an important job? Lamborghini could not have chosen better: In 1961, a technical and managerial upheaval had taken place at Ferrari. Several excellent engineers were attempting to rebuild their careers, one of them being Ing. Giotti Bizzarrini. Not only had Bizzarrini been involved in the development of the famous Ferrari 250 GTO that had

taken GT racing by storm in 1962, but he was also developing his own new designs of cars that would later be produced as the Chevrolet V-8 powered Iso Grifo and the Bizzarrini GT Strada 5300. He was a prolific engineer, for at the same time he also designed (though he did not produce) a 1.5-liter four-cam V-12 racing engine.

Lamborghini wasted no time in putting Bizzarrini on contract, commissioning a new engine design from him. Perhaps the philosophy behind the engine was no more complex than this: Ferrari's V-12s had 3.0 liters and a single overhead camshaft per bank, therefore Lamborghini's new V-12 would be bigger and better, with 3.5 liters and twin overhead camshafts per bank. Whatever its origins, the design was purebred and beautifully detailed from the start, forming the basis of the Countach's engine design to this day. Over the years the displacement has increased from 3462

Opposite page: Lamborghini's 350GT had a tubular chassis by Neri and Bonacini and a body by Franco Scaglione. The first prototype rolling chassis of the car was introduced in July of 1963, and the first deliveries of the front-engine car were in mid-1964. Above: The basic engine from which the rest of the V-12 Lamborghinis would follow was designed by Giotti Bizzarrini, beginning his development work in the early Sixties. The first Lamborghini V-12s displaced 3.5 liters and had double overhead camshafts per cylinder bank, with two valves per cylinder. The V-12's brake horsepower was rated at 280.

cubic centimeters to 5167 cc, four valves per cylinder have replaced the original two-valve layout, and the power has soared from 280 brake horsepower to 455 bhp, but the basic architecture has been maintained.

Once Lamborghini's first prototype had been built, the company hired 24-year-old Giampaolo Dallara as chief engineer to design and develop the chassis. Dallara's assistant was another young graduate from Bologna—Paolo Stanzani. While Dallara might seem to have been improbably young to take up the responsibilities of a chief engineer, he had a full degree in aeronautical engineering and had already spent four fruitful working years with Ferrari and then Maserati. He lacked no experience when it came to super autos.

Although Lamborghini would soon come to build a major proportion of his cars in his own factory, the manufacturing of parts for the original front-engined 350GT design was farmed out: The tubular chassis was by Neri and Bonacini of Modena, while the body style was by Franco Scaglione (formerly of Bertone), with construction by Carrozzeria Sargiotto of Turin. The gearbox was produced by ZF of West Germany and the final drive by Salisbury of the United Kingdom, while the brakes, wheels, and tires were all off-the-shelf proprietary items. The first prototype rolling chassis Lamborghini was revealed in July of 1963, followed by the first completed car's introduction at the Turin Motor Show in November of the same year. Deliveries of the front-engined 350GT began in mid-1964. The schedule would be a major achievement by any standard, but as far as Ferruccio Lamborghini was concerned, it was normal operating procedure.

In his own mind, Ferruccio was already working on another new design, one with a mid-mounted engine.

Above: The chassis for the first Lamborghini was designed by chief engineer Giampaolo Dallara and Paolo Stanzani. **Right:** The quality interior of the 350GT featured full instrumentation and many control levers. **Opposite page:** A special project Miura using zinc parts was built by Lamborghini and Bertone in cooperation with the International Lead Zinc Research Organization, which considered the Miura a "...spectacular sports car...produced by two of the world's most renowned figures in Grand Turismo car production...."

Miura:
Ancestor of the Countach

When the rolling chassis of the Lamborghini Miura was displayed at the Turin Motor Show in November of 1965, it caused a sensation. Surely, the pundits said, this upstart manufacturer Lamborghini could not be serious. How could any company, never mind one that had only been building automobiles for two years, consider building such a ferocious machine?

The Miura was the trend-setting exotic car design of the late Sixties, and it was the ancestor of the Countach. Not only was it a "first" in so many ways, but it made the entire concept of mid-engine supercars believable. Without the Miura, some say, no Countach would ever have come about. Without the Miura, the entire generation of mid-engine cars might have been delayed for several years. The Miura — or Project P400 (where **P** stood for **Posteriore** or rear-mounted and **400** for the 4.00-liter engine), as it was known at first—broke new ground in many ways. Not only was it the first road-going automobile to have its engine placed behind the seats, but it was the first such car to place a massive V-12 engine in that position as well. So much of a sensation might not have been caused if the engine had been placed in the

normal longitudinal position, as in the racing sports cars like the Ford GT40 and the various Ferrari prototypes, but the Miura had the unexpected and startling configuration of the 350-brake-horsepower powerplant being mounted across the chassis. The V-12 completely filled the wide space behind the passenger cabin.

The Miura was Dallara and Stanzani's first masterpiece, with a design that was altogether more pure and forward-looking than either of the original 350GT and 400GT Lamborghinis had ever been. Wherever one looked on the Miura, indications of the future could be seen. Although the all-independent coil-spring suspension was conventional by most accepted Modena/Maranello standards, the rest was new. The chassis was a pressed and fabricated platform unit, where most competitors still were using multi-tube layouts. The engine was not only behind the seats and mounted transversely, but was mounted with an all-Lamborghini-design five-speed transmission. Carrozzeria Touring was already preparing to produce a body shell. The name **Miura** was taken from that of a particularly notable type of fighting bull, one of many such names to be used for Lamborghini models

through the company's history. The connection between Lamborghini and bulls came about because Ferruccio Lamborghini's astrological birth sign is Taurus, and he also had long been an afficionado of Spanish bull-fighting.

After burning a great deal of midnight oil, the first completed Miura was shown at the Geneva Salon in March of 1966, and even more innovation remained to be seen. Following the financial collapse of Carrozzeria Touring, Lamborghini formed an association with Bertone for the first time. Bertone's chief stylist Marcello Gandini lovingly shaped the sensuous lines of the two-seat Miura coupe. Among the Miura's detail features were headlamps that were not covered behind panels (as would later be the fashion), but lay back staring sightlessly at the sky, neatly aligned with the sweep of the front fenders. Operating the headlight switch caused the lenses to rotate forward and upward, where they then operated at the minimum legal height for European cars of that time.

The first deliveries of the Miura were made at the end of 1966, changing the face of the super auto business. The car convinced the world of motoring in general and Lamborghini's

Right and opposite page: Ferruccio Lamborghini's Miura made the entire concept of mid-engine supercars believable. It was the first road-going automobile to have its engine placed behind the seats and in front of the rear wheels — a massive 4.0-liter V-12 engine, at that. The rolling chassis was introduced in November 1965, and the first bodied car in March 1966. Bertone's chief stylist Marcello Gandini shaped the Miura's lines. The name Miura is taken from that of a particularly notable type of bull, and it was in keeping with Ferruccio's Taurus astrological birth sign and his love of bull fighting.

rivals in particular that the brash new company meant business. Through the next six years, about 750 Miuras of three distinct types were built. Not only were they among the world's most exciting cars, they gave Lamborghini a great deal of experience in the manufacturing of such exclusive machines. All Miuras were phenomenally fast, of course, certainly causing Ferrari to take a look at itself. Not only was the original Miura faster than the Ferrari 275GTB/4 of the period, but it also looked more advanced, and it sported the now-fashionable mid-engine layout. As for Maserati, the Miura made its front-engine cars look old-fashioned, though Giugiaro's styling on the Ghibli made up for that at the time.

For the record, the P400S of 1970, having 370 bhp (DIN) in European-market tune, was good for 172 miles per hour. It could sprint from rest to 60 mph in 6.7 seconds and to 100 mph in about 15 seconds. Maximum speed in second gear: 86 mph; in third: 121 mph; in fourth: 153! That was all very well for those interested in only speed statistics, but a Miura owner had quite a bit more to learn about the car than that. The high-performance car had rather hair-raising properties in terms of aerodynamics. High speed could cause the nose to go light and the front to lift. French road tester Jose Rosinski, who has driven most modern Grand Prix cars and who is not given to exaggeration, is convinced that a test car that he was driving took its front wheels off the

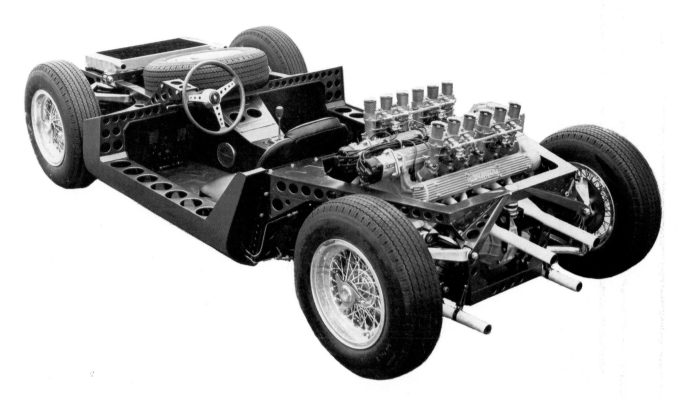

ground at one point and that he was lucky not to get involved in a horrible accident. Even so, most independent testers lucky enough to come into contact with a Miura, including Lamborghini's own American-born tester/development engineer Bob Wallace,

were able to achieve maximum speed without having the need for a pilot's license.

Another problem that the Miura had was its difficult handling characteristics when traveling at or near the limit of tire adhesion. Lamborghini's

conflict in producing the car was in giving it handling and road-holding characteristics acceptable to expert drivers trained for speed yet making it comfortable enough for the rich and untrained drivers who tended to buy the car. Experts needed a firm ride

Opposite page, top: The Miura continued many of the practices that were begun in the first of Ferruccio Lamborghini's cars — full instrumentation, for instance. Bottom: Details of the Miura's styling and design portended things to come, both from Lamborghini and other carmakers. Above: The Miura chassis without a body reveals details about engine placement and frame construction. Left: Thanks to the 370-bhp 4.0-liter V-12, Miuras were phenomenally fast, capable of a top speed of 172 mph and 0-60 mph in 6.7 seconds.

with rapid steering response in order to get the most out of the Miura, while the millionaires wanted ease of drivability in an exclusive automobile that they could use for show. Engineers resolved the problem well enough, but most observers now agree that the Miura could be "difficult" when driven hard or pushed at all beyond normal driving ranges. If an inexperienced driver entered a corner too hard (not unusual with the colossal performance available), he tended to lift off the throttle abruptly, causing all manner of torque reversals in the driveline and tires. The result could be a rapid spin in an uncontrollable

2900-pound automobile. While reaping the benefits of being the first to field a mid-engine super auto, the company also had to go through all of the development problems.

Even at the height of its fame and while selling like hotcakes at the rate of 200 units a year, the Miura still didn't have competition from Maserati or from Ferrari. Neither company had even started to design an answer to it. Lamborghini, however, never doubted that it could improve on the Miura. By 1969, the first sketches had been made that would result in the birth of the now-legendary Countach in the early Seventies.

Top: A detail from the door of the Miura — this piece of work preceded many of today's similar "innovative" designs by more than 20 years. Above: The Miura's body sections are low in number and large in size. Opposite page, top to bottom: Lamborghini's symbol is a bull in a dramatic attitude. Bertone's is a bit more stylized. The result of Lamborghini's Project 112 and Bertone's styling has become better known as LP500 or the Countach.

Project 112
and the Bertone Connection

That the Countach took time to mature as an automobile should be made very clear from the start. Begun in 1969-70 as an experimental show car and revealed to the public in March of 1971, delivery of the first Countachs to customers did not take place until 1974. A great deal of work, and then a great deal of reworking, was involved during that five-year span.

Whereas the Miura had been Giampaolo Dallara's labor of love, credit for the Countach goes to Paolo Stanzani. At the end of the Sixties, an important personnel change had taken place at Lamborghini, for technical chief Dallara had no longer been able to resist the siren call of motor racing and had moved on to develop a new Formula 1 Grand Prix single-seat race car for Alejandro de Tomaso. Even in the mid-Sixties, Dallara had hoped to see Lamborghini pursue motor racing, and from time to time he and engineer Bob Wallace had dabbled with the idea of an ultra-light Miura being driven in long-distance sports car events. However, Ferruccio Lamborghini himself would never sanction such a program. Dallara's move to de Tomaso (later to free-lance for Lancia on the very successful Stratos rally car project) meant that Lamborghini needed a new design chief. Ferruccio made the very bold decision to appoint Stanzani as chief engineer and plant manager at Sant'Agata, a plant that was now building more than 400 cars every year.

Almost immediately, Stanzani started a new project, along with his young assistant Massimo Parenti. They gave the project an anonymous and rather unimaginative code number — 112. Two years would pass before the designation **112** gave way to **LP500,** and the name **Countach** came after that. The bare bones of the design, incidentally, took shape at about the same time that the "ultimate" Miura — the SV variant — was being developed and while design work on the smaller Lamborghini — the Urraco — was also proceeding, so the small technical office suffered from no lack of work through the period.

Truly, the apprentice had become the maestro, for the Countach was a masterpiece. Everything that the design team had learned from the Miura and from its front-engine four-seat sister car — the Espada — was used in the design of the Countach. Ferruccio Lamborghini trusted Stanzani's judgment in the same way that he had allowed Dallara to produce the original Miura, and Ferruccio apparently did not interfere in the analytical work that led up to the birth of the new car. Stanzani's objectives, in any case, were logical and clear-cut: He wanted a car that was as advanced for its day as the Miura had been, and he also wanted to ensure that the car had better weight distribution, roadholding, and handling than that of the Miura. Furthermore, Stanzani was convinced that the new car had to have better high-speed aerodynamic qualities and that it should be altogether easier to drive than the Miura.

The easier-to-drive objective was the one that produced the major change of design layout between the Miura and the Countach. Although the Miura had been somewhat of a miracle in packaging due to the use of a transversely positioned V-12 engine and an integral transmission, the design gave the car a rather low polar moment of inertia. While the Miura had the ability to change direction rather easily, once the limit of tire adhesion had been passed, that direction change could rapidly transform into an uncontrollable spin. However, these inherent characteristics were not to prevent Project 112 from having a mid-engine design. But to give the new car an easier-to-drive profile, Stanzani decided to mount the engine and transmission parallel with the line of the chassis rather than perpendicular to it. The shift of the engine by 90 degrees relative to the chassis line demanded close attention to two major considerations: One was that the Lamborghini engine was very long, and the other was that Stanzani was not proposing to mount the gearbox in the conventional position.

Invariably, an inline mid-engine mounting results in the engine lying ahead of the line defined by the rear wheels and axle, with the final drive between the wheels and the main transmission in the tail, behind the axle line. Ford had designed its sports-racing GT40 that way, and Lotus had done the same thing with the Europa, as had Porsche with the VW-Porsche 914 and 914/6 coupes. Stanzani's solution was as mechanically elegant as it was different. The massive V-12 engine was placed in the fore-and-aft position, but it drove forward to the five-speed all-synchromesh transmission that was neatly placed under a high and bulky tunnel between the two seats ahead of the engine. The differential assembly behind the engine was then driven by a solid driveshaft running back alongside the engine's crankshaft in a sealed lubrication chamber separate from the engine's crankcase. The differential assembly was in a long casting that also doubled as the sump pan. Almost automatically, one expected that the arrangement was going to make the Project 112 car at least longer, if not wider or heavier, than the Miura had been. However, published figures contradicted those expectations. The Miura's wheelbase had been 98.6 inches and its overall length 171.5 inches, whereas the Project 112 design had a wheelbase of just 96.5 inches and an overall length of 163.0 inches. Lamborghini had learned quite a bit about packaging in just a few short years, with Project 112 confirming the theory that a well-designed V-shaped engine of six, eight, or 12 cylinders, complete with all of its accessories and manifolds, tends to be as broad as it is long.

The other remarkable feature of the new car was its styling. Lamborghini had once again relied on Bertone and its design chief Marcello Gandini for the styling of the new project. To compare the Countach style of 1971 with that of the Miura of 1966 is to illus-

The capabilities of Ferruccio Lamborghini's automaking company were honed through its design and development work on the Urraco (left) and the Espada (below) automobiles, along with the development that had taken place on the Miura. The Urraco was the company's first four-seat mid-engine car, introduced in 1970. It had a 2.5-liter V-8 engine in a body designed to be able to accept a front- or mid-engine mounting. The Espada was the Miura's sister car, a four-seat two-door having a V-12 mounted in the front.

trate just how far the fashionable shape of super autos had moved in five years. Whereas the Miura had been rounded, with flowing lines and an almost feminine feeling, the new car was altogether sharper, more aggressive, and more masculine in its stance and manner. Project 112's plane-like styling was flatter than the Miura's from the front to the rear wheel arches and onto the rear. The rear deck was flatter. The layout of the doors and their unusual opening geometry was one of the most arresting styling features: Instead of opening in a more conventional manner (sideways from front-mounted hinges) or in the gullwing configuration (upwards as the Mercedes-Benz 300SL or the De Lorean DMC-12), the doors of Project 112 tilted up from the back, swiveling upward and forward past the line of the windshield pillars. There they stood like an insect's upraised wings. Bertone had first shown the unique door-opening treatment on

the Alfa Romeo-powered Carabo show car of 1968, and that the Carabo's sensational basic lines and proportions could be seen in the Project 112 car was no coincidence. The shape of the front end was in keeping with the rest of the car: The hood rose from a very low, sharply chiseled nose to the base of the windshield, where the window glass picked up the lines at almost the same angle. The styling was a departure, for all previous Lamborghinis (even the Miura) had maintained a distinct difference in slope between sheet metal and glass. From the peak of the windshield, the body lines began to sweep gently downward again. At the sketching stage, a proposed periscope rearview mirror had its sight line immediately over the top of the engine bay cover. Apart from the much sharper angular style, the principal front end difference between the Project 112 car and the Miura was that the headlamps were completely hidden from view behind

covers until needed at night. At the rear, the lighting took the form of taillight clusters that were trapezoidal in shape, fit into the sharply cut-off tail of the car. The original design had no built-in spoilers or other aerodynamic aids. Bertone's Gandini had once again outdone himself, and clearly he had relished tackling a project where the client had not interfered; then he had smoothed out the extreme details and generally toned down the treatment for Lamborghini.

Through the initial design sketches and plans, and then through to the stage of building the wind tunnel model, the engineering and styling concepts for Project 112 were coming together as an obvious masterpiece. The problem now was to carry through and turn Stanzani's super auto dream into an exotic reality.

While Bertone's Marcello Gandini was working his magic on the shaping of the new Lamborghini project, Paolo Stanzani's small team was

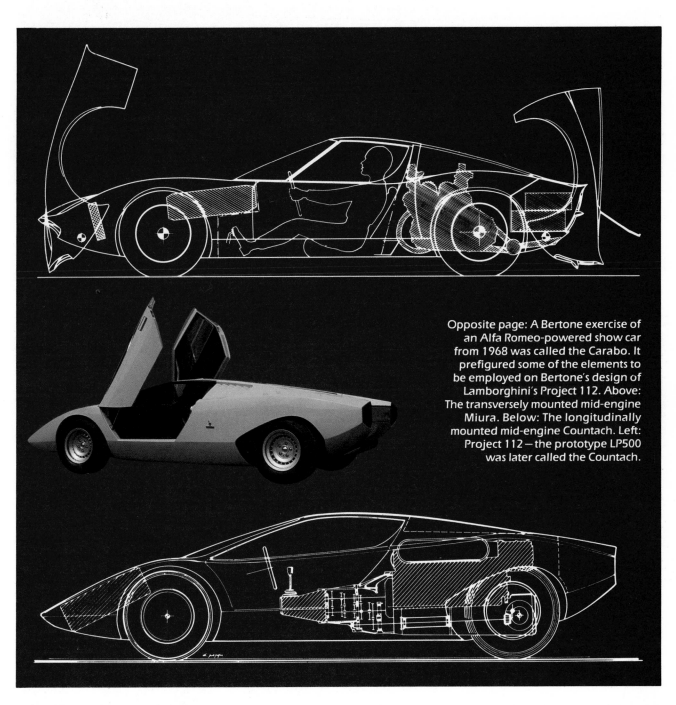

Opposite page: A Bertone exercise of an Alfa Romeo-powered show car from 1968 was called the Carabo. It prefigured some of the elements to be employed on Bertone's design of Lamborghini's Project 112. Above: The transversely mounted mid-engine Miura. Below: The longitudinally mounted mid-engine Countach. Left: Project 112 — the prototype LP500 was later called the Countach.

developing the car's engineering features at Sant'Agata. By this time Project 112 had taken on a new title — LP500. **LP** stood for **longitudinale posteriore,** an Italian expression referring to the longitudinal mounting of the rear-positioned power unit, and **500** anticipated the use of an exciting five-liter version of the famous Lamborghini V-12 engine. The one proposal was retained throughout the project; the other was dropped eventually.

The chassis of the very first LP500 was simple and straightforward, because it wasn't intended as the production prototype at the point of its construction. Its uncluttered design used square-section tubing with steel panels welded to various faces. The chassis could be referred to as semi-monocoque rather than platform. Despite the temporary nature of the prototype chassis, it did allow a basic format to be established. By using modified Lamborghini steering and suspension units from the existing parts bin, the working frame enabled the company to display a functioning show-car release rather than having to exhibit a non-running mockup. That the first LP500 show vehicle had a running chassis shows the amazing ability of an enthusiastic Italian automobile design team. All of the experience accumulated from working with the Miura series was reflected in the choice of suspension and other chassis parts. The Miura had independent front and rear suspension by coil springs and double wishbones; so did the LP500. The Miura had rack-and-pinion steering without power assistance; so did the LP500. The Miura had Girling disc brakes at the front and rear with vacuum servo assistance; so did the LP500. The Miura SV used 7.5-inch wide wheel rims in the front and 9.0-inch rims in the rear; so did the LP500 (naturally, both cars carried the latest 70-series Pirelli V-rated tires).

The major engineering design effort in the early stages went into the layout of the engine and the transmission—a layout unique not only to Lamborghini but to every other carmaker in the world. To talk about mounting a massive V-12 engine back-to-front and arranging a transmission to operate closely around it is one thing, but to accomplish the task properly is definitely another. Lamborghini managed it magnificently. With the LP500, Lamborghini proved just how versatile its engine was and how resourceful its designers and engineers had become. In only a few years, the famous V-12 had found itself used in three distinctly different attitudes: With all the front-engined cars, the engine had been conventionally positioned with the flywheel/clutch facing to the rear, whereas with the Miura the whole engine had been transversely mounted behind the seats with the flywheel/clutch facing to the left side. Now, with the LP500, the engine was in the longitudinal position once again, but it was in the rear with the

flywheel/clutch facing forward. In each case, a suitable transmission had to be bolted to the engine, and in each case different sealing and lubrication problems had to be solved. Such problems would be tricky in the development of any new car, but in the case of the Lamborghinis, the problems were made more severe by the extremely high forces of acceleration, braking, and cornering that would be employed, causing oil to surge. Even so, a dry sump system was not needed, and all of the indications have been that the standard installation that came to be used in the LP500 was sufficient to handle the job.

As the LP500 took shape, concerns about future engine exhaust emission regulations around the world made Lamborghini look at its V-12. To ensure outstanding performance in the future production cars, the show car's engine had to be changed: The 385-brake-horsepower 3929cc engine of the Miura SV was not enough, despite its being the most efficient road car engine in the world at its time, providing the Miura with a top speed of more than 170 miles per hour. Accordingly, Stanzani proposed a 4971cc version of the V-12, for which the factory conservatively quoted 440 bhp (DIN) at 7400 rpm and 366 pounds-foot of torque at 5000 rpm. Compared to contemporary V-8s of American manufacturers, the figures don't seem that impressive, but two differences should be considered: First, figures from the United States seemed to have a degree of built-in optimism, being quoted in SAE gross horsepower, which was much higher than DIN figures. Second, the Lamborghini figures were lower than had been seen in the testing of the engine.

The larger-displacement V-12 had a bore of 85mm and a stroke of 73mm, compared with 82mm and 62mm for the earlier four-liter unit. All in all, it was now a powerful monster—so powerful, indeed, that the company had some concern about the longevity of the engine and its castings. The LP500 engine's cylinder block and

light-alloy sump were new and specially cast for its longitudinal placement in the car. Not only did the sump have additional longitudinal ribbing to aid in the cooling of the oil, but it also incorporated two separate chambers. The one to the rear, having a separate end-on cover, enclosed the hypoid bevel final drive assembly with its limited-slip differential, while at the side of the crankcase was a long tunnel for the output shaft from the gearbox to the final drive. The forward-mounted five-speed gearbox had a remote-control linkage sprouting even further forward. With the engine and transmission taken out of the frame and turned about, they looked normal for a front-engined car except for the strange lump ahead of the engine where the final drive was located.

The 440-bhp engine of the super auto had to be cooled, of course, and Stanzani proposed using two radiators. However, they were not to be placed to the front of the car, but one on each side of the engine bay with air intakes located in vents behind the doors' glass. Whether or not such a placement would work satisfactorily was a matter of conjecture during the design phase, because no experience with such placement had been gained from the Miura or any of the other previous Lamborghinis. The Miura's front-mounted radiator had been entirely different.

Putting all of the pieces together for the very first car took time, and perhaps Stanzani was relieved when the work could not be finished in time to be shown at the Turin Show of November, 1970. That allowed another Lamborghini to capitalize on the publicity—the smaller-engined P250 V-8 Urraco made its bow at that time. Work on producing the body at Bertone's workshops in Turin went on for weeks, into February and March of 1971. In the end, test driver Bob Wallace had to drive the precious prototype to reach Geneva overnight, where it was cleaned up in time to be displayed at the Geneva Motor Show in March. Literally no time had been

available for testing, for the chassis had been delivered from Sant'Agata to Bertone by truck. The only road experience was in the miles that Wallace had driven while crossing the mountains from Turin to Geneva.

In the meantime, the car had been named. According to popular legend, the name came about quite by accident. Until the last minute, apparently, no one at Lamborghini or at Bertone had thought about putting any name on the show car other than LP500. Then one of the workmen who had been asked to help complete the car for the Geneva show is reputed to have taken his first look at the beauty and exclaimed, "Countach!" The expression is a typical Piedmontese Italian one for which no exact English translation is possible. The word **Countach** might best be translated to mean "Jeez!" in American English; suffice it to say that the car's name stems from a forceful outburst of Italian slang.

By the end of March, 1971, the

dream had become a reality. Lamborghini's Project 112, which had been renamed LP500 and was now the Countach, was on display at the Geneva Motor Show. How would the world react? How would Stanzani's and Gandini's masterpiece be received?

Top: In March of 1971, the world was shown the first Countach at the Geneva Motor Show. It has set the standards for exotic cars for more than 15 years. Above: The prototype had a five-liter V-12, later to be reduced to four liters in size.

23

Dream Car to Production:
The Evolution of the LP400

Critics, needless to say, were amazed by the Countach show car. All over Europe, magazine editors strained to procure the best photographs and to learn as much as they could from the sparse information provided by Bertone. The Countach, after all, was on the coachbuilder's rather than Lamborghini's stand. Such a move furthered the impression that it was only a dream car.

Autocar, Great Britain's authoritative weekly magazine, was so thrilled with the Countach that a complete two-page layout of the car at Bertone's stand opened the feature report on the Geneva Show. Little else needed to be said. **Motor** wrote that "...the greatest excitement was created by Bertone's confection based on Lamborghini components....Rear vision is restricted to a small periscope let into the roof, but with 440 Lamborghini horses for propulsion, what goes on behind isn't too important." **Autosport** simply called Geneva a "coachbuilders' dreamland" and commented that "...one could write pages about Bertone's V-12 Lamborghini.... Though possibly a one-off, the car is beautifully finished, with elaborate finned light-alloy castings everywhere.... The whole car is full of new ideas which repay the closest study."

One of those ideas, which had been a Bertone rather than a Lamborghini invention, was the interior treatment, particularly the instrument panel. At first, Bertone had wanted to use a complete "space-age" display, with digital readout speedometer and tachometer. The idea never made the transition from artist's drawing board to reality. The LP500 prototype, as it appeared in the show, had conventional analog speedometer and tach, along with two large warning lights on the steering column — the yellow one for small problems and the red one for large ones, as was noted by one European Lamborghini authority. Instrumentation also included a crude form of cruise control, having orange lights close to the speedometer and tachometer arranged to light up as certain preset speeds were passed. The most intriguing feature, however, was a monitoring panel that had been positioned to the left of the driver's line of sight on the front wheel arch intrusion into the cockpit and close to the door hinge. The panel was arranged to show a schematic diagram of all of the car's various ancillary functions, and it was hooked up to pinpoint anything that was not working

correctly. Once again, Bertone had developed an early step toward electronic monitoring panels that now appear on many automobiles.

All in all, the cockpit was a little roomier than that of the Miura — perhaps four inches wider across the seats, with about an inch and a half more headroom and no less than seven additional inches longer in the footwells. At last, it seemed, a Lamborghini had been designed to be driven by people of more than average height.

The pros and cons of the new en-

gine and radiator layout included observations that the front of the car would not be as warm as the Miura had been, but that the hard-working gearbox located between the seats might more than make up for that. Mechanically, however, the LP500 Countach could not impress until independent testers had been allowed to drive it, and that was not likely to happen for many months. The astonishing aspect of the Countach was its looks and design, with the unique door-opening detail and the mechanical layout of the engine and transmission. Everyone seemed to be bowled over by the car's sharp-edged style, very low and very wide by European standards — the essence of a square-hipped and ultra-powerful bruiser, rather like the Ford GT40 and its imitators. At 41 inches in height, the LP500 was just a tad taller than the GT40, but the Bertone body had a substantial width of 74 inches. The LP500 was an unbelievable car, one which few spectators could conceive as being practical for road use. It was

something over which to exclaim (remember "Countach!") and something perhaps to covet, in the manner that a collector might drool over a Picasso painting or an Epstein sculpture. But was it the sort of machine to be used in heavy traffic every day? It might easily impress the millionaire neighbors when parked outside one's home in Grosse Point, but how would it cope with a smoggy Los Angeles traffic jam, the temperature of a hot day in Dallas, or the rough and tumble of downtown New York City or Washington, D.C.?

The problem for Bertone and for Lamborghini was that far too many show-stoppers such as the Countach had been seen before. Whatever happened to the Carabo show car, for instance — the one that had inspired the styling of the Countach? And whatever happened to the luscious Ferrari-based specials produced by Pininfarina? Manufacturers' motor museums are full of one-off project cars that starred for a matter of months and were then quietly stolen away,

with their publicity-inspiring assignments successfully completed.

Although no one could guess at the time, this show car would be different. Even though Bertone had arranged to use the car for several static assignments after the Geneva Show, Lamborghini was anxious to get its hands on the car and develop the Countach into a practical, though formidable, road-going machine. Even though no firm production program and no actual intention to replace the Miura existed, the project was worth continuing as a technical and developmental exercise. Bob Wallace had learned enough from the single test drive from Turin to Geneva to realize that Stanzani's team had the basis right. Perhaps a lot had to be done and many changes had to be made, as with any prototype vehicle, but the team was on the right track.

As time went on, everyone wondered what was taking Lamborghini so long in developing the Countach for production. The Geneva show car had made such an impact that surely

Opposite page and left: The astonishing aspect of the Countach was its looks and design, with the unique door-opening detail and the mechanical layout of the engine and transmission. The problem for Bertone and for Lamborghini had been that far too many show-stoppers such as the Countach had been seen before. Whatever happened to them? Admirers awaited the fate of the car: Introduced in 1971, the first production Countach was not made until 1974.

Lamborghini would rush it into production, however limited the numbers might be and whatever the price would have to be paid for one. Not too many knew that no such plan existed at the time and that the whole foundation of the Lamborghini empire was distinctly shaky. As it turned out, the very first Countach delivery, to the Canadian oil tycoon Walter Wolf, was not to be made until 1974 — three years later. By no means were the entire three years spent in developing the Countach. But during that time, the engine size was reduced and the styling was refined, and the chassis design was completely rethought. When the Countach did not reappear during 1971, neither on Bertone's stand in London nor at the Turin show in November, onlookers readily assumed that it had merely been a show special after all. At the time, however, Lamborghini was at once trying to begin production of the newly announced P250 Urraco, begin prototype redesign of the Countach, and stay in business.

By 1972, the Lamborghini empire was in serious financial trouble, not because the car business was unsuccessful, but because of problems with Lamborghini tractors. A new factory at Pieve di Cento, still very close to Ferruccio's home, had swallowed up a large amount of capital, while a hoped-for order from the United States had collapsed. Eventually, Lamborghini had to sell the business to Saem, of Treviglio. The tractor company problems and the escalating expense of making the Urraco in quantity caused Ferruccio Lamborghini to sell 51 percent and effective control of the shares in Automobili Ferruccio Lamborghini to a Swiss businessman named Georges Rossetti. The sale was apparently worth about $2,000,000. An interesting wrinkle was that Rossetti not only controlled a lot of wealth, but was also a Lamborghini. Therefore, he must have known what sort of engineering and what sort of character were in the cars made by the company that he now controlled. Almost at once, Rossetti took up managerial control, Ferruccio withdrew from the plant, and Stanzani's work load was increased even more.

Meanwhile, Bob Wallace logged some very fast road miles onto the one and only LP500 prototype, confirming that the quickly designed chassis was surprisingly effective, that the aerodynamic behavior at high speed was considerably better than that of the Miura, but that a serious problem with overheating existed and that all manner of other work needed to be done. Altogether, the first long series of proving trials with the LP500 prototype showed great promise, including high-speed autostrada observation of the car's aerodynamic properties. Observers from another Lamborghini automobile photographed wool tufts stuck onto the body shell, showing the effects of wind on the car from various attitudes.

The major design problem with the car was that the cooling radiator layout could not keep engine temperatures in check. Much more air would have to pass through more efficiently placed radiators. The first radiators were positioned on each side of the engine bay longitudinally, with the air finding its way into that part of the car through the louvers behind the doors' window glass. Air slipped past the louvers rather than going through them, so the obvious solution was to provide differently shaped entryways to transversely mounted cores. Larger intakes were needed, and several arrangements were tried on the original car. Imagine Bertone's alarm at the sight of some of the crude scoops and slots that were tested. Although the final result must have been a compromise, the overheating problem was solved, and the styling wasn't entirely ruined: Two new intakes on each side of the car replaced the original louvers. One was an aeronautical-style NACA-shaped intake, which started in the doors below the handles and culminated several inches back, halfway between the rear of the door and the beginning of the wheel arches. The NACA intakes were not

enough. New scoops stood above Bertone's carefully evolved shape, taking the place of the original louvers and looking something like rectangular ears or sensing devices. No matter — the intakes worked, fixing the problem of overheating.

In the meantime, Ing. Stanzani's team decided to retain the same wheelbase, suspension, and basic mechanical layout of the prototype, but it set out to produce an even more

robust chassis. Logically, something sophisticated such as a true monocoque could have been expected, for several Italian super autos of the period were already so equipped: Maserati's Indy of 1969 had a unit-construction frame built by Vignale, as did the mid-engine Bora of 1971. Bertone itself was producing a monocoque for the new Maserati Khamsin. Lamborghini's own front-engine Espada used a pressed and fabricated platform frame. But

such a chassis was not chosen for the production Countach. Instead, Lamborghini designed one of the complex yet very rigid multi-tubular chassis for which the Italian metalworking industry was famous. Compared with a Ferrari Dino or a Daytona chassis, that of the Countach had far more separate tubes of much smaller diameter, being a piece of three-dimensional sculpture and ingenuity. To produce the chassis in quantity, Lamborghini

chose the company of Marchesi of Modena, a specialist chassis-building company used to thinking accurately in three dimensions. Marchesi was already building Jarama, Espada, and Miura frames in quantity for Lamborghini, so the Countach commission held no terrors.

In the meantime, some agonizing decisions had to be made about the engine. Everyone at Sant'Agata was nervous about using the full five-liter

Opposite page, top: Production LP400s retained the same wheelbase, suspension, and basic mechanical layout of the prototype, but had a more robust chassis. Bottom: Lamborghini designed one of the complex yet very rigid multi-tubular chassis for which the Italian metalworking industry was famous. Above: Scoops on the production Countachs stood above Bertone's carefully evolved shape, looking something like ears or radar sensing devices.

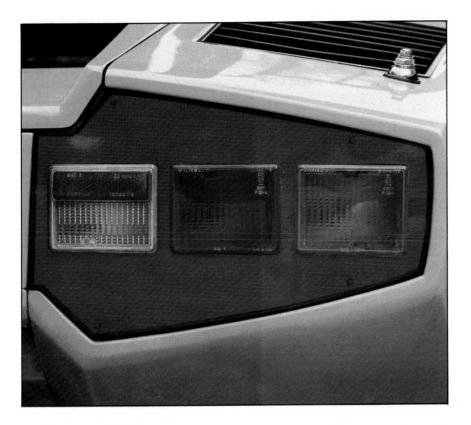

engine, and, in the end, they decided to revert to the familiar 3929cc dimension, even though it was a rather different engine from the others due to the number of unique castings and component differences involved. Because the engine size had been reduced at the development stage, the LP500 title of the prototype was abandoned, to be replaced by the LP400 label that was also to be the official title of all original Countach production cars. Lamborghini, however, was satisfied with the available power, and it advertised the car as being capable of 195 miles per hour, a figure that no independent tester ever approached.

In March of 1973, at the Geneva Show, exactly two years after the original car had made its sensational debut, a definitive preproduction Countach LP400 was put on sale. The car on display was a real Ferrari-baiter in its Italian red coachwork, and it was very different from the earlier LP500. The two-year development period had witnessed many subtle, often overlooked changes to the body style, the car's equipment, and its engineering. All of the changes were made in the interest of making the Countach easier to produce, more practical, and better equipped. One important factor was that for the first time a Lamborghini body shell would actually be assembled at Sant'Agata rather than by the coachbuilder responsible for the style. In the case of the Countach, individual pressings, foldings, and hand-formed panels would be supplied by Bertone, but assembly, welding, paint, and trim would be done in-house. Some of the inner panels were of steel, but much of the shell and all of the skin were of aluminum.

One important feature of the production Countach was that the fantastic facia panel, seating, and interior were abandoned, to be replaced by a neat but by no means advanced design. A complete center console enclosed the central transmission tunnel, the front end of which supported auxiliary instruments and switchgear. The steering wheel had become a normal three-spoke type, with the familiar Lamborghini Bull horn button at the center. Enclosed in a deep surround was a long, slim but otherwise unassuming panel displaying analog instruments. Behind the panel, an air-conditioning kit was fitted to cool down the interior in hot weather conditions.

Outside the LP400 prototype, the shape was still stunning — something that has amazed and delighted every true lover of fast cars for many years — but many improvements had been made. At the front, the side/turn indicators were out in the open, but headlamps were covered. The front hood was hinged from the nose, and the windshield wiper arrangement had undergone some development. In the side windows, the small slots had been retained, but the production LP400s would have larger slots covering about half of the window area. The air intake scoops for the radiators gave the car an even more machismo appearance than that of the LP500.

With some time left before the car was ready to go on sale, a second preproduction car was built, tested, and shown at the Paris Salon of October, 1973. Painted green, the car incorporated additional changes: a large, single, pantograph-action wiper blade; small rectangular driving lamps in the nose (that would have been useless at high speed); a different detail shape to the nose; and extra air intakes helping to channel air to the front brakes. Slowly, but definitely, Lamborghini and Bertone were developing the LP400 Countach, and it was losing the pristine, uncluttered looks of a one-off to become a practical sales proposition. In the rear, the production-specification car looked less exciting than the prototype had, mainly because no money was available with which to make tooling for the large trapezoidal taillights. In their places were flat metal panels with three rectangular lights or reflectors

on each side that looked as if they had come from a standard parts bin and could be bought from any Fiat dealer's parts department.

Finally, in the very depths of the Energy Crisis, the first true LP400 Countach production car was completed. Almost exactly three years after its predecessor — the LP500 — had been shown for the first time, the Countach was ready to go on sale. Only one final obstacle to its progress remained, and that had more to do with people than the machine's engineering. With the maturity of the Countach, not only did Bob Wallace leave Lamborghini, but Ferruccio Lamborghini chose this time to sell out his remaining shareholding of the company. Wallace, more than any other development engineer, tester, or driver, had helped to maximize the great character of Lamborghini automobiles. But with the selling of Ferruccio's shares in the business to Rene Leimer, and with his complete withdrawal from the business that he had set up in 1963, Lamborghini left some doubt if the company's future without him would be a real future after all.

Above: The LP400 production car was as stunning as the LP500 prototype. Improvements had been made, however. In front, the side/turn indicators were in the open, but headlamps were covered. The front hood was hinged from the nose, and the windshield wiper arrangement had undergone some development. The small slots in the side windows had been retained, with larger slots now covering about half of the window area. The air intake scoops for the radiators gave the car an even more machismo appearance than that of the LP500. Opposite page: The LP400 Countach was developed slowly but definitely, losing the pristine, uncluttered looks of a one-off concept or show car along the way to become something that could be sold in the automotive marketplace, albeit an exclusive portion of that marketplace.

The Countach Grows Up: 1974-1978

By the time the LP400 was ready to go on sale, it faced formidable opposition. Three years earlier, in 1971, it had still been unique. But now the Italian super auto industry had caught up with it: Maserati had started selling Giugiaro-styled mid-engine Boras in 1971-72, while Ferrari's charismatic 365GT4 BB finally went on sale in 1973. Even the optimistic though inexperienced proprietors of Automobili Ferruccio Lamborghini—Rene Leimer and Georges Rossetti—could see that the Countach had a battle on its hands in the marketplace.

Even so, the company was not planning on building many cars. Although the world's automobile markets may have collapsed in the wake of the Energy Crisis with its corresponding jump in fuel prices, the truly rich were as always—seemingly immune from economic disasters. They were standing in line to get their hands on a Countach. For some, no matter how influential, the wait was going to be a long one. Stanzani's work force, complete with tooling installed, was not really capable of building many more than 50 Countachs a year. More than that number had already been ordered. By the end of 1974, only 23 of the cars had left Sant'Agata. Partly, the low number was due to the complexity of the car and the fact that its body shell was actually assembled at the factory. Partly, the number was due to the deteriorating industrial climate in the business. Apparently, having an assured job in the Italian motor industry and being involved in the construction of the world's fastest production car were not enough for the artisans at Lamborghini.

The cost of the Countach was not holding back interested buyers, though it was astronomical by any standard. For instance, in politically neutral Switzerland in 1975, a Countach was listed at 115,000 Swiss Francs, compared with 119,500 SF for a Ferrari Boxer, a mere 81,100 SF for the Bora, and 78,650 SF for the newly announced Porsche Turbo. Even a standard Rolls-Royce Silver Shadow could be had for 111,200 SF. At any rate, the Countach was listed at a very high price. Lamborghini had no plans to send the Countach to the United States, and it was not carrying out a program to prepare it for overseas. The cost of such work for a tiny European manufacturer had shifted from being prohibitively expensive to ludicrous as the Seventies progressed.

All the frantic work needed to federalize the Urraco had made that very clear. At first, Stanzani took the view that any rich motoring buff determined to buy a Countach would also find a way of importing it into the U.S. as well.

By almost any standard, the assembly of a Countach was a time-consuming process: Very few mechanical aids were used, and a great deal of hand work was required. The body shell had to be assembled, painted, and trimmed, though the only manufacturing of running gear that was actually carried out by Lamborghini was the machining and assembly of the engines, transmissions, and some suspension components. The company had no casting or forging facilities of its own.

The complex, three-dimensional, multi-tube chassis frame arrived already painted from Marchesi of Modena. It was mounted on a trolley, which was pushed along the simple "assembly line," a U-shaped sequence of stations in the lofty factory building. The frame has been described as a thick-tube derivative of the famous Sixties-style Maserati birdcage frame, with an almost uncountable number of individual tubes, brackets, and gussets and their accompanying welded joints. Solid box-shaped lattices followed under the doors, and the frame had a lighter central backbone: Both the lattices and backbone surrounded the engine bay at the rear and supported the front suspension, steering, and spare wheel in the nose. Unlike the Ferrari Boxer, which used rather crude-looking but undeniably effective square-section tubes with no

Opposite page: On the surface, a Countach is pure glamor, sexy curves, and Italian **bravura.** Above: The Lamborghini company mascot.

35

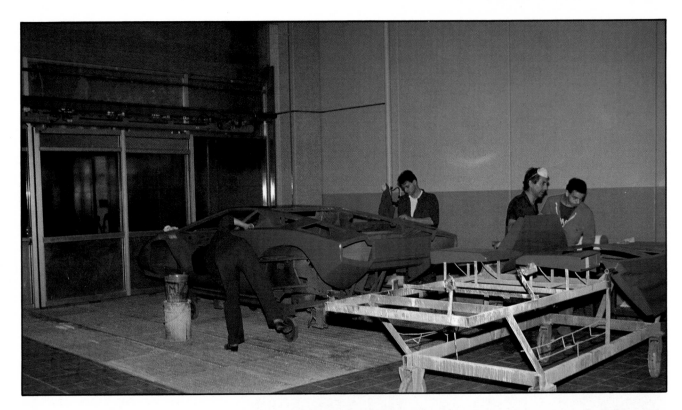

great frame depth to give beam stiffness, the Countach's frame was much more sophisticated and very rigid in all conditions. Countachs that have been crashed have stood up remarkably well to impact.

The body's undertray was fiberglass, but the majority of the body shell was composed of light alloys. Countachs under assembly wore a kind of assembly jig, the body support tubing being mounted and the panels being individually affixed, fettled, and fastened to the body frame. On the surface, a Countach was pure glamor, sexy curves, and Italian **bravura.** Underneath, ample evidence could be found of traditional metalworking crafts having been employed. The most difficult and complex job, no doubt, was to accurately assemble, hang, and adjust the vertically hinged doors and to get them to seal properly.

Detroit assembly lines can put together an engine at great speed and seemingly without effort. Compared with the assembly of an American cast-iron V-8, the scholarly and diligent manner in which a Countach engine and transmission took shape would have bemused an observer. Lamborghini's machine shops received steel and light-alloy castings and forgings from outside suppliers, then they

did their own delicate turning, shaving, milling, and boring before actual assembly could begin. The Countach engine had so much to go together: 12 pistons and connecting rods, 24 valves, two cylinder heads, six carburetors, two electrical distributors (not just one), a mass of high tension wiring, fuel pipes, and other items. The tubular exhaust manifolds themselves were a real credit to the Italian workman's craft. Every engine was completely assembled by a single craftsman, and every one was thoroughly power-tested before being fitted to a car. Many more man hours were

needed to complete a car, which would then be given a thorough test on the open road — throwing it into the reality of contending with trucks, Fiat 500s, horse-drawn carts, Vespas, and pedestrians. All of them make fast driving in Italy such an adventure. The autostrada close to Sant'Agata was a two-lane road and very busy, not offering much opportunity for extending a new Countach to its limits, either.

Even with the Countach line in full production, the best that could be expected was only a single example of the car finished every week, so the LP400 was always likely to be an ex-

clusive car, no matter what designs were in mind for it. With such production figures, very few early owners were likely to sell their Countachs at a loss if found unsatisfactory. (How on earth could the value of a one-owner, carefully driven, pre-owned Countach be established?) At this stage in the development of the car, Lamborghini's attitude toward the automotive press had perceptibly changed. Procuring a unit for a test drive wasn't easy. When Ferruccio Lamborghini himself had been in charge, the factory was almost like an open house most of the time. (The exception was in Bob Wal-

lace's "toy shop," where the secret prototypes took shape.) But during the Leimer-Rossetti period of ownership, the open-house policy altered considerably.

Luigi Capellini, once second-in-command to Alejandro de Tomaso in Modena, was brought in as managing director, not only to lend more experienced control to the building of such cars, but to try to restore the flagging fortunes of the Urraco, which had failed to make any impact on the U.S. market. During the time, the architect of the Countach, Paolo Stanzani, walked out, and he was replaced

Opposite page, top and bottom: The assembly of a Countach was a time-consuming process. Few mechanical aids were used, and a great deal of hand work was required. For instance, the body shell had to be assembled, painted, and trimmed. Top and above: Lamborghini carried out the machining and assembly of the engines. Steel and light-alloy castings and forgings from outside suppliers were delicately turned, shaved, milled, and bored. Then every engine was completely assembled by a single craftsman. Every one of the engines was then power tested in one of four buildings before being fitted to a car.

by Giampaolo Dallara—a familiar name at Lamborghini. Such a merry-go-round of personnel changing was quite normal in Italy. In the period since he had left Lamborghini, Dallara had worked with de Tomaso, with Lancia, and on his own.

While the availability of Countachs to journalists was practically nil because of exclusivity and price, some impressions were gained through various means. Lamborghini did not keep a demonstrator available. However, ex-Formula 1 driver John Miles tried out a privately owned LP400 Countach for Britain's **Autocar** in 1978. He wrote: "The Lamborghini Countach has always been something of an enigma not only in performance, but also in its road manners. Whether you like its looks or not, it must be the ultimate posing machine." After describing the unique mechanical layout, Miles commented: "This means that the main bulk of the engine sits pretty high. Compact describes the driving compartment. Noel Gibbs [the owner] might be comfortable, but there was no way a six-footer could sit without hunched shoulders and cranked knees....Oddly enough, once we started to move, some of the claustrophobic atmosphere disappeared. The centrally mounted gearchange was heavy, but the engine felt good, top end-y, and noisy too—it had a hard note that meant business. How quick? Difficult to say; it was certainly very highly geared in fifth—a gear too high to be used at all at Goodwood circuit.

"Cornering quickly but not sliding, the Countach gave me a spooky feeling as if there was a lot of weight in the rear that would be only too ready to take over pendulously and spin the car....Apparently both bottom rear wishbones were later discovered to be bent...." Miles, a very accomplished and analytical road-car driver, was clearly not happy with the handling of that particular car.

The other long-established British motoring magazine, **Motor,** was much more content with the car that it tested in 1975. The magazine recorded 149 miles per hour in fourth gear, beat 160 mph in top gear, but never attempted a maximum speed run. It estimated the top speed of the car to be something around 175 mph, though Lamborghini was still claiming top speeds of more than 190 mph. No doubt any car that could sprint to 100 mph in a mere 13.1 seconds would impress most testers, but **Motor** seemed to have been electrified by the sheer performance of the Countach, calling its acceleration "startling" and summing up the car by giving it many compliments: "The Countach was the best Lamborghini we've driven. Well engineered and shatteringly fast, this £18,000 [about $45,000] space-age projectile turned just as many heads as the Ferrari Boxer. If anything, it handled and stopped even better than the Ferrari, and had more luggage space. But the engine had nothing like the Boxer's flexibility, and visibility was poor, which made it even harder to drive in traffic."

Even so, the test car was another Countach that had less-than-perfect handling: "The suspension and steering are fully adjustable, which means that, within limits, you can set up a Countach to handle and ride as you wish. The factory normally adjusts the cars so that they handle as near neutrally as possible. Our car had its front track incorrectly set, though, a fault which made the Countach feel unstable under heavy braking and prone to oversteer when cornered near the limit. On the road, we had no trouble controlling the errant tail when it did step out of line, but within the safe confines of...[the] test track, where very high cornering speeds are possible, it would have been all too easy to spin the car." The biggest worry was what to do should the car roll onto its roof and the doors jam. **Motor** closed its report, "How do you get out if it rolls? You push the windscreen out!"

Road & Track's test of a privately owned Canadian car, published in February, 1976, resulted in an ecstatic review. The report was headlined, "The

Below: The layout of the Countach's five-speed manual transmission and engine places the shift lever at the front of the entire assembly. Opposite page: The Countach has inspired many quotable reactions—"Whether you like its looks or not, it must be the ultimate posing machine." "Being seen in a Countach is a real ego trip." "The Countach was the best Lamborghini we've driven. Well engineered and shatteringly fast, this...space-age projectile turned just as many heads as the Ferrari Boxer. If anything, it handled and stopped even better than the Ferrari, and had more luggage space."

fastest car we've ever tested." The engine was specified at the usual European level of 375 brake horsepower at 8000 rpm, and the testers loved the sensation of driving such a high-performance engine: "We have become so accustomed to low compression ratios, retarded timing, exhaust gas recirculation, surging, stumbling and like problems that we sometimes forget how it was in the good old days BS (Before Smog)...." The overall reaction to the car: "If you don't love cars, don't even try to understand the Countach. Its no-holds-barred,

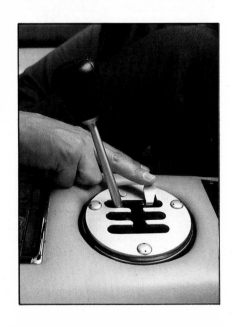

cost-no-object design is, on one hand, one of extremes and excesses and, on the other, a mobile demonstration representing the pinnacle of automotive design, technical achievement and sophistication, the likes of which we will probably never again see. We can think of few cars that are endowed with the emotional and visual charisma of the Countach. Its brutally angular Bertone body is striking from every angle. It has enough NACA ducts, scoops and vents to keep an aerodynamicist content for a lifetime. . . . But more than all those things, the Countach is an extremely well engineered car that has evolved from an idea car at Geneva in 1971. . . . Reading about a car is one thing. Seeing it in the flesh, driving it and testing it is an entirely different matter. We sometimes approach cars like the Countach with trepidation, fearing that it won't live up to our expectations. With the Countach we worried for naught. Just a few minutes behind the wheel was

enough to convince every driver that the Countach delivered everything it promised, and more."

The fact that the magazine tentatively estimated the price of the Countach in the U.S. at $52,000 in 1976 and that "we don't question its ability to pull 8000 rpm (192 mph) in top gear" didn't make the testers lose all sense of proportion. Obviously, a great deal of compromise had been exercised in the driving compartment: "Open the door, slide in (climb would probably be a more appropriate term as the door sills are very wide . . . and don't forget to duck your head) and you slip into a very comfortable body-hugging seat (being thin is a distinct advantage). . . . Being seen in a Countach is a real ego trip; but seeing out is another story. . . . Rear quarter vision is for all intents and purposes nonexistent. . . . Driving the Countach in traffic, especially at night, is intimidating, to say the least." Yet the Countach had so much character, so much well-

developed sporting and animal-like behavior, that the testors could forgive it almost anything. To end their test, they chose these words: "Very few cars, regardless of price, provide the spine-tingling thrills and excitement that driving a Countach provokes. Is the Countach the ultimate exoticar? Probably. Is it a perfect car? No. No car is flawless, and as we said before, the rear quarter vision is poor. But worst of all, the seatbelts are lousy."

All in all, that sort of impression was normal throughout the world of motoring. As the Countach very gradually began to appear on the roads of western Europe and very occasionally on those in the U.S. and Canada, it became less of a myth and more of a desirable artifact. The effect was almost as if a silver-screen goddess had stepped down from the movies, to be seen in the flesh as a real-life person. The image of the Countach was never harmed for the people who were buying the car, however. It was no

Above: Some super autos, indeed, were toys, but not the Countach. In every line of its shockingly stunning body, in every whoop of its magnificent engine, and in every chirrup of its tires, the Countach established itself as serious. Opposite page: Beginning in 1978, a new derivative of the Countach — the Countach S — was produced. Not only did it have a massive adjustable rear airfoil, a front chin spoiler, and wheel arch extensions front and rear, but it was also fitted with porthole alloy wheels and low-profile Pirelli P7s.

ordinary millionaire's car, and not at all the sort of thing that a pop idol or the heir to a dynasty would buy. Some super autos, indeed, were toys, but not the Countach. In every line of its body, in every whoop of its magnificent engine, and in every chirrup of its tires, the Countach made its character known: Forget the others. This car is serious.

One of the most famous Countach owners as well as one of the most faithful was Walter Wolf, a Canadian oil tycoon who drifted into the world

of Formula 1 racing in the Seventies. Not only did he buy the very first LP400 to be delivered to a customer in 1974, but he later had no fewer than three heavily customized examples, each of which was fitted with the same "personal" five-liter version of Lamborghini's V-12 engine. The combination of Walter Wolf and the return of Giampaolo Dallara to Sant'Agata eventually led to even greater developments on the Countach theme. After 150 LP400s, a Super Countach was on the way!

Maturity: The Countach LP400S and LP500S

Some day the entire Lamborghini story will be told—of what happened in the Seventies with its financial affairs and the personalities involved. But that time is not now. The twists and turns of fortune, the arrivals and departures of personnel, and the gradual crumbling of the fine automobiles for which Lamborghini had become famous are known only for what could be seen on the surface. The miracle throughout the period was that the Countach not only survived, but improved as the years passed. The Urraco might have flopped; the BMW M1 contract might have been lost; and the Cheetah

might have been stillborn. But the Countach marched on. The production of 40 to 50 cars a year might not be much of a basis for boasting, but the production rate and the quality of the cars themselves were consistent.

Beginning in 1978, a new derivative of the Countach—the Countach S—was being produced. In many ways, it was a much better, more mature car than the original. The two people mainly responsible for developing the S were engineer Giampaolo Dallara and enthusiast-customer Walter Wolf. Most of the modifications and improvements made

to the Countach to produce the LP400S had been developed for Wolf's "specials" or for one or two other discerning customers who wanted to make a great car even better. The first Wolf special was built in 1975, and it was obviously quite different from the ordinary Countach. Not only did it have a massive adjustable rear airfoil section standing on struts fixed to the bodywork behind the engine deck lid (to trim the rather light behavior of the back end at high speeds), a front chin spoiler, and wheel arch extensions front and rear, but it was also fitted with Lamborghini Bravo-style porthole alloy wheels and low-profile

Pirelli P7 tires. The five-liter V-12 engine, which was very rare and only on loan from the factory, gave the car even more outstanding performance than had the standard production four-liter engine. The second Wolf special was built a year later, and it had the same five-liter engine as before and all of the same type of extra equipment. The suspension was also further developed, and a public address system was installed so that Wolf could talk to other motorists without getting out of the car.

The essence of all of the specialized work, plus the continuing development of Lamborghini's own production cars, led to the company developing the Countach LP400S in time to be launched at the Geneva Motor show of March, 1978. The LP400S took over directly from the original LP400, which had already gone out of production before the new car was presented. Visually, the S was a bit of a shock, for although the original Bertone lines were still in evidence, a large number of add-ons had appeared, taking away some of the purity that many people had liked so much about the first models.

The chassis changes all centered about the new generation of ultra-low-profile Pirelli P7 tires. Because they

Body changes for the LP400S began at the front of the car. A deep snowplow type of chin spoiler flowed from the wheel arches forward and across the front. At the rear, fat wheel arch extensions curved out from under the already wide fenders, then abruptly cut off. The arch extensions front and rear served the purpose of covering the extra width of the portable wheels and Pirelli P7 tires beyond the point of the original wheel and tire location. The extensions were of molded fiberglass, whereas the rest of the body skin panels were manufactured from aluminum sheet. New badges at the rear let the curious know that here, with all of the changes, was the most recent Countach.

were so much wider and squat than previous-generation Pirellis or the Michelin XWX types that many LP400 models had used, the car needed different wheels with wider rims and reworked suspension geometry and settings. The Bravo-style wheels, with five portholes per cast alloy rim, now had 8.5-inch front rim widths with 205/50VR-15 Pirellis along with roller-like 12-inch-wide rear rims on which massive 345/35VR-15 Pirellis were mounted. Hidden away behind the wheels were different pickup points for the suspension springs and dampers, new suspension links and geometry changes, different stub axle

bearings, and a modified steering rack housing. In place of the original Girling brakes were ATE calipers front and rear, with larger discs. A few owners had found that they were able to punish their brakes to the point of deterioration, and the new brakes were meant to cope with all levels of demand.

Body changes began at the front of the car. A deep snowplow type of chin spoiler flowed from the wheel arches forward and across the front. At the rear, fat wheel arch extensions curved out from under the already-wide fenders, then abruptly cut off. The arch extensions front and rear

served the purpose of covering the extra width of the wheels and P7 tires beyond the point of the original wheel and tire location. The extensions were of molded fiberglass, whereas the rest of the body skin panels were manufactured from aluminum sheet. Without the new fiberglass arches, an LP400S would have needed either narrower tires or it could not have been driven legally on the road. New badges at the rear let the curious know that the vehicle ahead was a Countach of the most recent type.

On the other hand, no changes were made to the engine or to the transmission, though cold-air ducting

now directed fresh air from outside the car into the six hungry open-mouthed Weber carburetors. From time to time, the engine development team tried to produce versions of the engine that could be sold in the United States, but the first examples to be delivered in that market actually had engines prepared by Automotive Compliance Inc. As far as the casual observer was concerned, the most obvious changes turning the LP400 into an LP400S were the wheels and the body styling.

Walter Wolf bought the very first LP400S, and he instantly had it modified as he had his earlier specials. His

Left: The Lamborghini Bravo-style wheels, with five portholes per cast alloy rim, now had 8.5-inch front rim widths with 205/50VR-15 Pirellis along with roller-like 12-inch-wide rear rims on which massive 345/35VR-15 Pirellis were mounted. Hidden away behind the wheels were different pickup points for the suspension springs and dampers, new suspension links and geometry changes, different stub axle bearings, and a modified steering rack housing. Above: The LP400S Countach — even more fantasy.

Above: The miracle throughout the Seventies was that the Countach not only survived, but improved as the years passed. The production of 40 to 50 cars a year might not be much of a basis for boasting, but the production rate and the quality of the cars themselves were consistent. **Opposite page:** As a result of the emissions controls, the original four-liter V-12 engine of the LP400S had been progressively detuned. To counter the insidious power loss, the LP500S had been developed. While it was not the original Countach engine of five-liter size, it was yet another combination of bores and strokes. The 4754cc V-12 developed 375 bhp at 7000 rpm.

first S had the familiar large airfoil, plus it also had adjustable brake balance and anti-roll bars, along with unique eight-piston brake calipers from Automotive Products of the United Kingdom.

Soon after the launch of the LP400S, further financial and corporate upheavals took place at Sant'Agata. For some time, Walter Wolf seemed to be prepared to buy the business, with draft contracts for a share purchase from Rossetti and Leimer actually having been written. But nothing came of the sale. Eventually, with liabilities far exceeding assets, Automobili Ferruccio Lamborghini SpA was put into a type of receivership—a "controlled administration" arrangement with the Italian government, starting August 1, 1978. Dallara had gone, as had Capellini, so government administrator Dott. Artese performed a real coup in persuading the eminent Ing. Giulio Alfieri to join the company as engineering and production manager. Alfieri had become known for his exploits at Maserati. He in turn persuaded Artese to continue and even to expand the assembly of Countachs, whereas the long-running front-engine Espada four-seater was dropped.

Soon, however, the West German Hubert Hahne and his associate Dr. Raymond Neumann got involved in Lamborghini, and for a short time they seemed to be the new controlling shareholders. Whatever actually did happen, their control was short-lived. Then at the beginning of the Eighties the French-Swiss Mimram group took over. At the time rumor had Ferruccio Lamborghini buying back into "his" company. During this difficult period, a mockup of a turbocharged V-12 Countach engine was shown, but very likely such a unit was never run, and it certainly was never developed by Lamborghini.

Sanity eventually returned, and further progress was made on the Countach. What later became known as the Series 2 LP400S was introduced toward the end of 1979, featuring a modified facia panel incorporating

larger instruments and road wheels of simpler style. The adjustable rear airfoil, still optional, found its way onto most cars built past this time.

In the early Eighties, Lamborghini finally began sending Countach models to the U.S. However, some of the striking looks of the car were lost due to the addition of front and rear bumpers, Ferrari 308 taillights, structural stiffening around the passenger compartment, and beams in the doors to meet federal requirements. To keep the performance up to accepted Lamborghini standards, the engine had to be enlarged to 4.4 liters, but emissions controls took the hard edge off performance.

From the spring of 1982, the European-specification LP400S gave way to the LP500S. Still recognizable as the same amazingly attractive Countach on the surface, the LP500S was different under the skin. To meet ever-tightening exhaust emissions standards in many countries, the original four-liter V-12 engine of the LP400S had been progressively detuned, the result being only 350 brake horsepower at 7500 rpm. To counter the insidious power loss, the LP500S had been developed. Work on the larger-capacity V-12 engine had continued through the Seventies as one obvious way to counteract the stifling effects of government-regulated emissions controls. Lamborghini wanted to develop a larger engine that would hold together. The five-liter engine eventually used in the LP500S was not the original Countach engine of five-liter size, but yet another combination of bores and strokes: The 4754cc V-12

developed 375 bhp at 7000 rpm. Reductions had been made in compression ratio, and although the same Weber carburetors were used, the peaks of both the power and the torque curves had been reduced. Most of the increase in the capacity of the cylinders came from lengthening the stroke—one reason that the new engine did not rev as zestfully as the old.

About the only visual change to the car was to the outside rearview mirrors. Also, the tail carried a new

badge—5000S. The wheel arch extensions, wheels, taillights, and all the other aerodynamic aids remained.

Even though the LP500S was not quite as exuberant a racer as the Countach of the early Seventies, it remained a phenomenally fast car, as Britain's **Autocar** magazine was able to prove in the autumn of 1982. The testers traveled to Italy to try out the brand new car. By that time, the Mimram concern had renamed the business Nuova Automobili Ferruccio Lamborghini SpA, though little else had changed. If anything, more Countachs than ever were being produced at the Sant'Agata plant. **Autocar** was dismayed at first to find that the test car had a mere 149 miles on the odometer. Thinking that the low mileage

would mean a very stiff car that had not been broken in, the testers were assured by factory personnel that normal test procedures for each and every Countach V-12 engine had been followed on theirs as well: "It was explained that whilst a Countach with 3000 miles behind it would certainly be up to 500 rpm faster in top speed, the considerable amount of bench test running before installation ensured that the unit was at any rate initially run in. Each V-12 has six hours of being driven by an electric motor as its first breaking-in treatment. It is then started up and worked against a brake at various constant rpm between 2000 and 6000 in 1000 rpm intervals, at 1½ to two hours for each speed, after which its maximum power and torque

are measured to ensure that the engine is up to specification. Lamborghini are by no means a big company, especially now in their leaned-down, but apparently more efficient size, yet they have four fully equipped engine test houses in which this power unit preparation—two days of it—takes place."

The importance of the road test by the long-established and authoritative British magazine **Autocar** was that a pair of extremely experienced testers

meticulously did the work and recorded every statistic. (**Autocar** was the magazine that had stirred up a hornet's nest by suggesting that the Ferrari Boxer, at least according to them, could never be as fast as Ferrari claimed, and they also had figures to prove it!) **Autocar's** testers had no trouble in finding a flat, straight, and traffic-free stretch of roadway on which to go for the maximum, saw the tachometer needle settle at around 6700 rpm in top gear, and timed the car between carefully measured posts. They were happy to announce a top speed of 164 miles per hour, an announcement that brought the usual skepticism about testing methods on the one hand and wild claims from the factory on the other. But most sensible observers took the test at face value, allowed for the fact that a fully loosened-up LP500S might gain another 500 rpm and correspondingly gain 176 mph top speed. Ultimately, the observation was that yet another "speed barrier" existed at around 180 mph—a barrier yet to be breached by a super auto.

The top speed of the car, in any case, was not the most significant observation made about the LP500S: "Straight stability at maximum speed is reassuringly good, in spite of a suggestion of lightening steering...." Another observation was that the handling of a car properly prepared by the factory was extremely safe: "The car's ideal weight distribution, and its typical mid-engine low polar moment of inertia are largely responsible for its wonderfully balanced cornering. There is just the right amount of understeer to preserve stability,...which predominates in a high speed bend most reassuringly. Use the throttle and a low gear in a slow bend and the tail can be powered out, pleasantly controllable....Roll is hardly discernible. ...The Countach rides more absorbently than you might expect, but it obviously isn't a car to be taken over large bumps if one can avoid them." The acceleration, as you might expect, was still sensational, with 0-100 mph

being recorded in a mere 12.9 seconds, with 128 mph available in third gear and 152 mph in fourth, and with an overall fuel economy figure of about 12 miles per gallon to remind everyone of the profligate nature of its character. The testers headlined their report "King of the Supercars."

No wonder the queue to buy a Countach did not shorten in the next two or three years. The car, quite obviously, was as much of an animal as it ever had been, and, more importantly, it obviously had the very best roadholding and braking qualities to match the outstanding performance and extroverted looks. Even so, some things never changed on the car or couldn't be improved: It had always been awkward to climb into and out of, and once in place tall drivers were going to be uncomfortable, with heads hitting the headliner or with a knees-up driving position and thighs uncomfortably close to the steering wheel.

The performance, naturally, was sheer magic to the enthusiast, but it was achieved at the expense of very high engine noise in the cabin, a lot of rumble from the immensely wide Pirelli tires, and restricted luggage and storage space. Nevertheless, if you could afford to buy a Countach (near $100,000) and afford to insure it, then stand the high cost of routine 6000-mile service, it was a car to make any older person feel young, any average driver feel like an expert, and any true expert driver feel like a world champion. Also, the powerful visual attraction of the car was bound to transfer to the driver.

In short, perhaps the Countach **was** the "King of the Supercars" after all. Or was it? Giulio Alfieri and his team had not been idle since the Mimram takeover. An even more spectacular Countach was being developed, and in 1985 it made almost everything else look obsolete!

Opposite page: The Countach gauges continued to be of the analog type. Left: The optional rear wing increased road adhesion of the Countach but decreased its top speed. Above: "The car's ideal weight distribution, and its typical mid-engine low polar moment of inertia are largely responsible for its wonderfully balanced cornering. There is just the right amount of understeer to preserve stability . . . The Countach rides more absorbently than you might expect, but it obviously isn't a car to be taken over large bumps. . . ."

Super Countach:
The Quattrovalvole

When Lamborghini launched its latest Countach in March of 1985, the company made a very sweeping claim. The 5000 **quattrovalvole**, it said, was "the world's fastest production car": No **ifs**, no **buts**, and no qualifying phrases. The company was sure that it was the fastest. Perhaps Ferrari was lucky that it had introduced its own new Testarossa in the autumn of 1984, for without a similarly startling car, the latest **quattrovalvole**

Lamborghini would have had absolutely no competition at all. The latest version of the Countach was quite literally the sort of car about which enthusiasts fantasize.

The **quattrovalvole** looked the same, of course, but it had so much more power and so much more torque that the car's performance had taken a significant leap forward. No longer was the engine a relatively tame V-12 struggling to reach a maximum speed

The Lamborghini Countach 5000 **quattrovalvole** was touted as "the world's fastest production car." Here was a car that bellowed its power to the world, determined to breach the 180-mph barrier.

of 170 miles per hour. Here was a car that bellowed its power to the world, and it made determined efforts to breach the 180-mph barrier.

For most ordinary motorists, the difference between a 140-mph, a 170-mph, or a 180-mph top speed is purely academic because none of them are likely to experience it in an automobile. Even the very few rich people of the world who might buy a Lamborghini or a Ferrari aren't likely to check out top-speed claims, especially with their own cars. A monstrously high top speed is more of a symbol of power, a benchmark, or a statistic to bandy about. Better yet, it's a number to hold quietly in reserve for meaningful conversations. A car with such a high price tag had best be able to stand

behind the claims of its being the world's fastest super auto by being able to provide proof, should its owner have the nerve to try and should the highways provide the space. That, of course, is the great problem with owning a truly fast car in the mid-Eighties: Where do you let it all out, all the way to the limit? In Europe a person can try quite legally in West Germany, where the autobahns are unlimited, but where the traffic is also quite heavy. Italy has autostrada speed limits, but traffic is lighter in the south and the Italian police take a more relaxed view of Italian super autos being driven with exuberance. But nowhere else.

Nevertheless, Lamborghini felt that it had to make a major leap forward,

for it was not at all anxious to surrender the title of "World's Fastest" to Ferrari without a fight. The Miura that was produced in the mid-Sixties had certainly been the fastest, but Ferrari's Daytona had pulled ahead by the end of the decade. Some say that the original Ferrari Boxer was faster than the Countach LP400, whereas the LP500S was certainly quicker than the five-liter Boxer. Then, in the early Eighties, Lamborghini learned that the 48-valve Testarossa was on the way. Lamborghini knew that it had to surpass the Testarossa. So Patrick Mimram gave Giulio Alfieri permission to produce what some still call the Super Countach. Neither the money nor the time was available for the development of a completely new automobile. Like

Ferrari's parameters with the Testarossa, Lamborghini would modify and improve existing machinery instead.

The chassis of the revised Countach was left alone almost entirely, as was the body shell. Visually, indeed, the car looked the same as ever, except for some differences in the engine bay cover. The speed-sapping airfoil was still offered as an option and not included as a standard fitting.

In the engine compartment could be found the revisions of consequence. Alfieri had been Maserati's top man for a quarter of a century, during which the marvelous range of V-8s for all production cars and the V-12 four-cam racing engine had been developed. He and his new colleagues at Lamborghini relished the challenge of

making the Lamborghini V-12 the most powerful engine in the industry. Alfieri's solution—and a logical one by all the usual engineering tenets affecting engine design—was to make it burn more fuel/air mixture. To do so, the engine had to be given a greater swept volume and more efficient breathing. Boring out the engine would have been the easiest way to increase displacement, but, like Dallara and Stanzani before him, Alfieri knew that the cylinder bore had been pushed to its practical maximum. Therefore, any increase would have to come from a longer stroke. The revised engine, then, retained the 85.5mm cylinder bore of the existing LP500S, but the stroke was increased from 69mm to 75mm. Displacement

Opposite page: The chassis of the revised Countach was left alone almost entirely, as was the body shell. Visually, the car looked the same as ever, except for some differences in the engine bay cover. The speed-sapping airfoil was still offered as an option and not included as a standard fitting. Above: The Super Countach's interior didn't change much from those that had gone before, either.

55

went up to 5167cc. The Super Countach's engine had a stroke/bore ratio of 0.877:1 compared to the original Miura/Espada engine's 0.756:1.

Perhaps the much-changed engine was not going to soar to high revs as gloriously as the original had done, but it was certainly going to breathe more deeply. Alfieri's team threw away the original Fifties-style two-valve heads with their part-spherical combustion chambers and their vertical inlet ports sprouting between the cam covers. Then they started from scratch. The team left alone the block, the bottom end, and the back-to-front transmission layout. But the heads and carburetion were entirely new, with castings exquisitely detailed and machined, just as would be expected from Lamborghini. The heads featured proper cross-flow breathing, four valves per cylinder with a pent-roof combustion chamber shape, and an entirely fresh carburetor layout. The exhaust ports were on the outside of the heads, and the inlet ports pointed into the center of the V shape. Naturally, that left no space for the horizontally mounted Weber carburetors. In their place was a centrally mounted cluster of six downdraft twin-choke 44 DCNF instruments. Because of the new carburetion treatment, with the air box on top of them, the new engine looked taller than it really was. Two lengths of flexible air ducting led out to the flanks, aiming to pick up fresh air from the same position as it had been picked up on previous Countachs. The result was impressive, not only by comparison, but by absolute standards. An increase of only nine percent in swept volume produced a peak power boost of 21 percent and extra torque of 22 percent, giving the Countach quattrovalvole 455 brake horsepower at 7000 rpm and 369 pound-foot torque at 5200 rpm.

The world didn't have to wait long to discover how effective the new engine was, for Britain's **Autocar** was given an opportunity to test the car to its limits. The results, even from a new car having logged only 1100 miles,

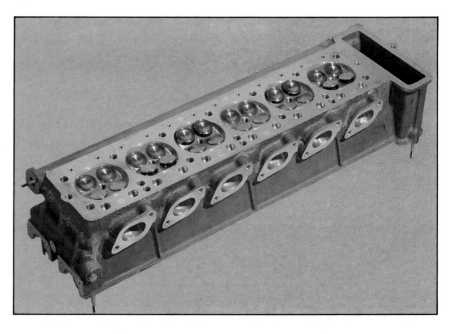

were astonishing. **Autocar** headlined its seven-page report "The Raging Bull" and its cover gushed, "178 mph — The incredible new Countach — Our fastest ever Road Test!" And so it was. The previous best mean speed had been the 174 mph recorded by a Ferrari Daytona in 1971. The Miura P400S had been good for only 171 mph. The previous 1982-model Lamborghini LP500S had produced 164 mph. Information "leaked" from the ultra-high-speed test track at Nardo, in southern Italy, suggested that a well-broken-in 5000 **quattrovalvole** ought to achieve 183 mph, and that the Ferrari Testarossa was not quite as fast. No wonder **Autocar** opened its article lyrically: "There's 7200 rpm on the rev-counter, and still the needle climbs. The concrete is flying under the short blind nose as we pierce the perspective taper of the road ahead. There is something a little end-of-the-rainbow-ish about what seems the real possibility that we are fast enough to reach the vanishing point at the end of that taper.... The car is rock stable in spite of a small lightening of the steering. Still no other being in sight, and still the long movement accelerator is flattened at the end of its travel. The needle is hovering now, on around 7300 rpm, and not rising any more. We hold the speed, waiting to make sure it really has stabilized — yes, yes, that's it.... 'It,' the highest fifth gear rev-counter reading we've seen this morning, turns out to correspond to 179.2 mph, the highest one-way maximum speed from any production road car **Autocar** has tested."

Nor was that all, for the **quattrovalvole** had not only produced an exhilirating top speed, but a fierce set of acceleration figures. The 0-100 mph sprint was down to 10.6 seconds, which was astounding enough, but the car then leapt on to reach 130 mph in 18.5 seconds, 150 mph in 25.1 seconds, and 170 mph in a mere 44.7 seconds. The last mark, astonishing as it was, came up in just 1½ miles of flat-out acceleration. The wonderfully rejuvenated V-12 engine was also amazingly flexible. **Autocar** always records the time taken to jump through 20-mph intervals in top gear (30-50 mph, 70-90 mph, and so on). On this occasion, the forward surge was more or less constant from 30 mph on up to 130 mph, in fifth gear. Accelerating from 30-50 mph took 5.8 seconds, compared with 70-90 mph in 5.7 seconds and 110-130 mph in 5.8 seconds. The effect, apparently, was like

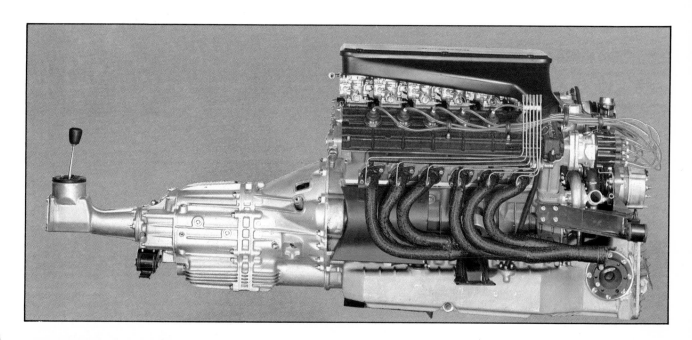

being on a free-fall run, but in a horizontal direction.

The Countach 5000 **quattrovalvole** had not only become the fastest production car in the world, but was still one of the most flexible. Short of driving the car, grasping how a machine capable of near 180-mph speeds could potter through the crowded suburban streets of an Italian city at 30 mph in fifth gear and then accelerate away smoothly when the road

cleared would be difficult. Nor would it be immediately obvious that the **quattrovalvole** could handle the 55-mph speed limit of the U.S. in every forward gear. Yet it could.

Giulio Alfieri is apparently convinced that a good deal more is possible from the basic Countach concept. Should rumored information be believed, the company's next attack will be on the styling of the car and its aerodynamics. Whatever next from Sant'Agata?

Opposite page: The heads of the **quattrovalvole** featured proper cross-flow breathing, four valves per cylinder with a pent-roof combustion chamber shape, and exhaust ports on the outside. Top: The Super Countach's engine displaced 5167 cc, and it developed 455 brake horsepower at 7000 rpm and 369 pound-foot torque at 5200 rpm. Above: Rumors have Lamborghini working on the styling of the Countach for better aerodynamics, trying different airflow techniques.

An Appeal to Fantasy

The Lamborghini Countach is aptly named, for the impression that it makes on the senses is startling. Everything about it astounds and amazes, and those who gaze upon it have to wonder if this car has anything to do with reality. As is the case with any automobile that is in some way different, the Countach has an undefinable mark of fantasy about it. Although the Countach is made of metal, fiberglass, and rubber, it has been set apart from others of its kind. It dares to be different. It proudly parades its uniqueness, which transfers to anything associated. The Countach is as bold a statement as any automaker has ever made, breaking the restrictive bounds of reality to show the world one person's fantasy and to offer it for sale to anyone who can afford the exotic. That fantasy—that super automobile—appeals to the joy we take in such incredible machines.

Born for the USA
The Lamborghini Countach wasn't always sold in the United States, so versions were not always prepared to meet United States emissions and safety regulations by being fitted with the proper exhaust equipment, bumpers, or door bars. Opposite page, top: Some things look awkward on a Countach, such as rear tires that are closer to a more normal size than the P7s. Bottom: Early U.S. front bumpers interrupted the flow of the Countach's lines. Top: A new Countach **Quattrovalvole** sits at rest without the rear U.S. bumpers installed. Middle: The most recent attempt at meeting federal bumper regulations looks like four black pads that are spaced across the back of the car. Bottom: The front bumpers that are fit to meet U.S. regulations give the Countach somewhat of a lip.

Customizing the Countach

Over the years, many Countach owners have wanted their unique autos to be made even more so at Lamborghini and afterward. Extra wings, side moldings, custom wheels and tires, and even more performance from engines have been given to base Countach models. Walter Wolf began it all with his custom wings, wheels, and engines. Right: Four-point harnesses are additions. Below: Note the side sills and **Turbo** lettering. Opposite page, top: The rear wing began with Wolf's cars. Bottom, left: Twin turbocharging makes a hot engine even hotter. Bottom, right: Scale Countachs from Agostini Autojunior of Italy are priced at more than some full-scale cars. This junior super auto boasts a tubular chassis with a fiberglass and Kevlar fiber body, a 300cc one-cylinder Briggs & Stratton engine, 11 bhp, and a 28-mph top speed.

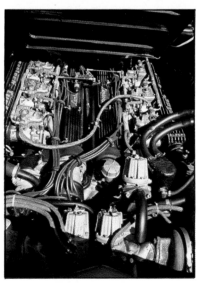

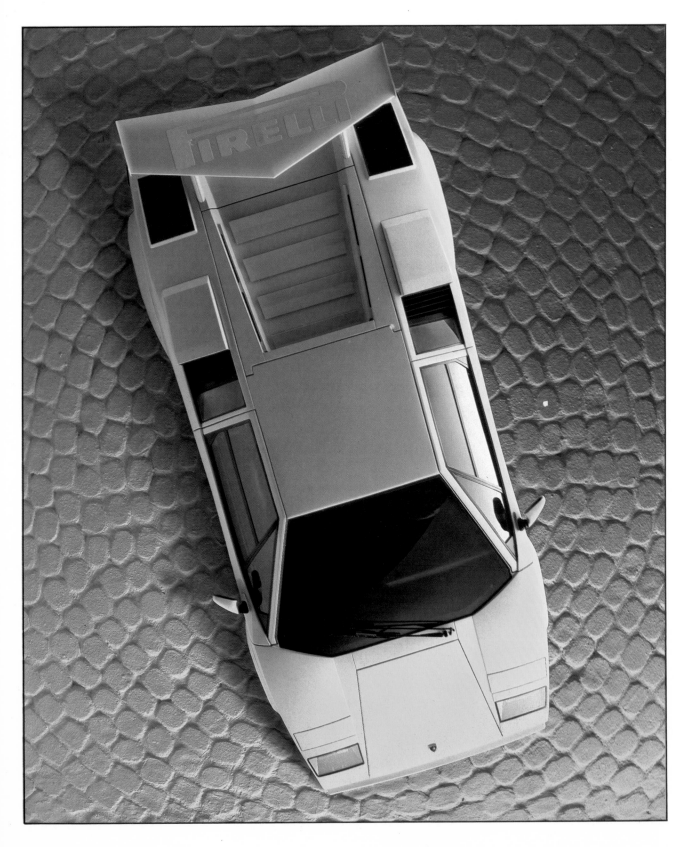

Marketing Appeal
By association, Lamborghini's Countach has been used in television and print ads to help sell many kinds of products, often ones not at all related to automobiles. The car is an attractive and alluring background. Here are ads for some products that are auto-related in nature. Opposite page: A Pirelli tire ad features a unique high-angle view of a Countach. Pirelli has something at stake in Lamborghini's effort, in that its huge P7s are the Countach's rubber meeting the road. Above: Alpine Electronics capitalizes on Lamborghini's use of its stereo equipment. Left: This Countach is of smaller scale than most — a 1/12-scale model produced by Tamiya and distributed by MRC.

Lamborghini Countach Specification Chart

General: Multitubular chassis frame, with separate steel and light-alloy body shell. Mid-engine, rear-drive, two-seat coupe						

Model	Miura SV	LP500 Prototype	LP400	LP400S	LP500S	5000 Quattrovalvole
Production	150*	1	150	385	325	160/year
Dimensions and Capacities						
Wheelbase (in.):	97.7	96.5	96.5	96.5	96.5	96.5
Overall length (in.):	171.2	163.0	163.0	163.0	163.0	163.0
Overall width (in.):	69.4	74.4	74.4	78.7	78.7	78.7
Unladen weight (lb.):	2739	2910	3020	2915	2915	3188
Drivetrain						
Engine type:	2 ohc 60° V-12	2 ohc 60° V-12	2 ohc 60° V-12	2 ohc 60° V-12	2 ohc 60° V-12	2 ohc 60° V-12
Mid-engine position:	Transverse	Longitudinal	Longitudinal	Longitudinal	Longitudinal	Longitudinal
Displacement (cc/ci):	3929/239.7	4971/303.2	3929/239.7	3929/239.7	4754/290.0	5167/315.2
Bhp (DIN) @ rpm:	385 @ 7850	440 @ 7400	375 @ 8000	375 @ 8000	375 @ 7000	455 @ 7000
Lb/ft torque @ rpm:	294 @ 5750	366 @ 5000	268 @ 5000	268 @ 5000	302 @ 4500	369 @ 5200
Compression ratio:	10.7:1	10.5:1	10.5:1	10.5:1	9.2:1	9.5:1
Transmission:	Five-speed manual	Five-speed manual	Five-speed manual	Five-speed manual	Five-speed manual	Five-speed manual
Chassis						
Suspension:	Independent, coil springs, shocks	Independent, coil springs, wishbones, anti-roll bars	Independent, coil springs, wishbones, anti-roll bars	Independent, coil springs, wishbones, anti-roll bars	Independent, coil springs, wishbones, anti-roll bars	Independent, coil springs, wishbones, anti-roll bars
Steering:	Rack-and-pinion	Rack-and-pinion	Rack-and-pinion	Rack-and-pinion	Rack-and-pinion	Rack-and-pinion
Brakes:	Four-wheel disc	Four-wheel disc	Four-wheel disc	Four-wheel disc	Four-wheel disc	Four-wheel disc
Tires and Wheels						
Front:	FR70VR-15	205/70VR-14, 7½" rims	205/70VR-14, 7½" rims	205/50VR-15, 8½" rims	205/50VR-15, 8½" rims	205/50VR-15, 8½" rims
Rear:	FR70VR-15	215/70VR-14, 9" rims	215/70VR-14, 9" rims	345/35VR-15, 12" rims	345/35VR-15, 12" rims	345/35VR-15, 12" rims

*Total production of P400 Miura, P400 Miura S, and P400 Miura SV: 765 units